The LIbrary of Disposable Art
Volume One
David Macpherson

Introduction to the Library

I have been lucky enough to write a column in the Worcester Magazine for over two years now. My work only comes out once a month, which is just the right amount for me. This book has the first two years of the Library of Disposable Art.

One day, in February of 2020, I complained on Facebook that I miss writing a column. I used to write one for GotPoetry.Com and I did a blog called Gin and Tonics Across Worcester, but I treated it like it was a column. I had a great time with those two ventures and I said I would like to do a column, but I had no place to do it and no idea for it.

Usually, that kind of complaint, where the would be artist complains about not doing their art, is ignored.

But this time, my friend Victor made a comment, saying, "Worcester Magazine is looking for people to write columns and commentary." Now, one should understand that Victor is the editor of the Worcester Magazine.

And like that, I had someone willing to let me try to write a column. One problem. What the hell do I write about?

For a few years, I have been writing short books about pop culture. I wrote one of the books about one episode of the New Scooby Doo Movies. Another of the books was a second by second examination of a Tom Petty music video. Another looked at the Perry Rhodan book series. Very obscure, and a lot of fun. When I wanted to brand them, I came up with the title "The Library of Disposable Art."

When faced with coming up with a column to write, I thought of this series and it materialized in my mind quickly. I will do ones that cannot sustain an entire book. The first one that I knew I wanted to do was about coloring books.

Over the February vacation, I wrote the first seven and sent them to Victor. They have been in the magazine every month or so since then.

Every few months I will recall that there are only a few columns waiting and I will sit down and write a few more.

They seem to be well received. We even got a piece of fan mail. Yes. Just one. But in this day and age, to have someone hand write and send a letter is pretty amazing.

When I run out of interesting, or at least funny, topics, I have gone to my friends in a trivia group and they have given me ideas. Thank goodness.

It should also be said that the first column came out just weeks before lockdown. Some of the pieces are about going and looking at items at shops, which no one was allowed to do for months. In some ways, the lockdown sparked interest in collecting things. And that seems to have helped interest in what I was creating.

Now, you should know that it was Victor who decided which ones were published. Some of them were never published. I don't know which ones they are. I was never good at making sure that it was put in print or not. I really should have paid more attention, but I am sure there was an interesting video on YouTube to distract me.

I hope you enjoy reading all of them, the good and the bad. For some, I will be adding some comments and updates. But that's enough of me talking about the column, let's just get to the damn thing already.

David

March 22, 2021

One: Coloring Books

Welcome to the Library of Disposable Art. We are the collection of art that was never meant to be seen or contemplated for more than a glance, like comic strips. It includes things that were never meant to be art, but people love it and keep it all the same, like beer bottles.

Today, I would like to start with the best example of disposable art, the coloring book. Let me clarify, up until ten years ago, the coloring book was in the land of "for kids." We got to give Cousin Mary's son a present when we visit, let's get him a coloring book. Kids like coloring.

We should talk of the adult coloring book and its goal of mindfulness. But if you look at a completed page done by an overstressed forty year old accountant living in Millbury, every section is meticulous and perfectly ordered. That might be nice to calm his frayed psyche, but really, where the hell is the fun in that? Where are the messy smudges and crossed over mistakes? No. Let's stick to coloring books for children.

First question, why do we think that all kids like coloring? We make them color. But do they like it? Of course the way we want them to color is too specific to be fun. Color in the lines. You have to be careful to use the right color and to stay in the marked off areas. School psychologists will wonder what's wrong with you if you scribble with abandon.

Coloring books are not about a finished work. It is a process. You don't look back at the coloring book you have attacked and contemplate it for years to come. As soon as all the pages are filled with crayon trails, then that coloring book is finished. There is no reason to keep it. Toss it out. It is full. Time to get another coloring book to draw on and forget. Coloring books are a temporary fix.

We parents might be impressed with our toddler's first completed page of color and cacophony. We give them a big kiss and adhere it to the fridge door with a magnet. The Fridge Door, the child's first art museum. But then soon enough, those coloring book masterpieces are replaced with the menu to the Chinese restaurant that delivers, which is a different kind of disposable art. We love what the little ones do, but after a while, it's just color inside and out of the lines.

And what coloring books do we give them? That doesn't help. Superman. Scooby Doo. Barbie. Bratz. Care Bears. Snoopy. Happy Days. Ghostbusters. Transformers. The things we think they like. We saw Timmy watch Ben 10, he must want to push a crayon over his likeness. It is the facsimile of enjoyable pastimes.

How often did you get a coloring book when you were home sick from school?

It's a throw away. It is a killer of an icy snow day. Kids can be so proud of the Jackson Pollack explosion they put on the line drawing of Garfield and Odie. But they will still turn the page and color the next one. And the next after that. Coloring is a volume activity.

Now I collect a bunch of disposable art. I have original comic book art. I have art that was made for children's books and comic strips. In the case of comic strip art, I love the idea that all of this beautifully detailed work was made just to be reproduced in the newspaper once and only once. I used to spend a good deal of time loitering on EBay, looking for the best bargains for this type of forgotten creation.

But in my collection, the thing that has pride of place are the original art from coloring books. I love having them. They are not pretty things. They are just the pen and ink outline of the action that will be filled in by the kids at home. They are simple things. I have original art from Little Lulu, Blondie and I Love Lucy. I stare at my Fantastic Four coloring book art. I even have all the art for a coloring book that was to teach kids how to be safe on the playground. Of course, the best way to teach kids these rules is to have an anthropomorphic moose and his pals play and cavort. There is no plot, no sequential momentum in these books. It is snapshots of a story that does not fit together.

My wife thinks I'm crazy. She can't understand why I would want these things.

I love the idea of coloring book art. The original art. An artist spent hours or days creating pages of art that was meant to be defaced. They create just enough for the four year old to take over. "Don't worry, I got it from here."

What an exciting thing for an artist to contemplate. They are the inspiration for a thousand interpretations. No finished coloring book page is like any other of the same page. Everything is original. Every page of Strawberry Shortcake playing with her friends is a chance to create something amazing, something with colors we should not expect. Art that ignores lines and rules is the art that we might get a chance to create while killing time during a rainy summer's day or anxiously waiting in the front room of the doctor's office.

Two: Community Theater Programs

What is the difference between memento and artwork?

While looking for something else in my teeming attic of doom, I found a small pile of programs to plays I attended. I must have kept them. Why would I do that?

There are around forty or fifty of them. They start around 1997, when I lived in Somerville, and go towards 2007 or so, when I was married and living in Worcester. I have continued to see theater, I just stopped bothering holding onto the folded piece of paper they gave me when I entered the black box performance space.

These are simple objects. Most are double sided xeroxes made late at night at Kinkos (I really miss the 24 hour copy shops). Most have no illustrations on the cover. They are just pretty fonts discovered on an early version of Word. Some have simple line drawings. Like the cover for the Hovey Players production of the Nerd. We see an illustration of a guy in suspenders sitting on a giant roll of toilet paper. I am sure this is somehow explained in the play. Or maybe not. Maybe someone just thought this looked funny.

These are hastily made pamphlets given out when you enter the play. They are time killers to look at while you wait for something to start happening. They are prompts for memory. They focus me to remember what the play was, what I was at the time.

There is the neon yellow program for K&K Productions of The Trial of the Catonsville Nine. It was performed at WAG, which is now the Sprinkler Factory. I remember there were no stage lights, so everything was performed with the usual overhead lighting. Where I stood in the back, I noticed someone had left a copy of the play lying about. As the actors performed their lines, I followed along, noting when they messed up a word or reversed a line. This is a memory I did not have a minute before. Looking at the seventeen year old program allowed me to recall that.

That program has pictures and bios of each of the performers. There is a headshot of Mike Duffy, who played the judge. He was an amazing folk singer. I saw him a lot and I loved hearing him every time. He passed away in 2005. I don't know when was the last time I thought of him.

There is the cheaply made program for WPI's production of Return to Forbidden Planet. It was a silly play melding Shakespeare's The Tempest with the old flick Forbidden Planet, all with fifties do-wop songs. I remember liking the robot on roller skates. The actor was having a hard time staying upright through her solos. I didn't want to go by myself, so I talked two friends into going with me. They didn't know each other. They spent the entire play whispering to each other and tentatively holding hands. After the play they decided to go for a drink, I think they forgot to invite me. They started a short, but memorable relationship that evening. I wonder what they recall of the play.

The cover to the playbill for Stage Loft's production of Dirty Work at the Cross Roads, doesn't have the play's title on it. You have to go into the program to find out what you are seeing. My wife and I, just married, went to see it. It was an old 100 year old melodrama with a Snidely Whiplash bad guy and a damsel tied to the tracks. They handed out popcorn with the programs and encouraged us to throw popcorn at the bad guy and shout hurrah when the hero appears. The popcorn is gone, the program remains.

There are many other pieces of paper that tell stories not written by any playwright. I Hate Hamlet. The Smell of the Kill. Black Coffee. Escape Artists Don't Bake Brownies. Black Mariah. You're a Good Man Charlie Brown. 42nd Street. The Skin of Our Teeth. Roadside America. Some of these have strong memories. Some of these are just words I typed out for you.

The jury is out if this is disposable art, or just things that are disposable. Can programs for community theater make the leap up to art? I'm not quite sure, but they do for me what good art can: they elicit emotion, they make me think of long gone friends and the fleeting joy of entertainment.

All the programs and concert ticket stubs that we keep in shoeboxes. They might not be art. But they let us recall the art we once were.

Three: Video Cassette Box

The last VCR was manufactured in 2016. That means there are still VCRs out there ready to take care of all your video cassette needs. But there is a finite number that one can actually use. The amount of VCRs will only diminish.

But what is the good of them now that they have crashed right into the wall of obsolescence?

For the most part, you will not be able to watch the videos that you have in a box in the closet. If you want to watch Die Hard, then you can watch it on DVD or whatever streaming service has it. I do know that some rare cult movies are only available on VHS and some serious lovers of obscure horror films will spend some good money for such a treasure. But that is not the usual route.

You can still buy them at That's Entertainment. At Jelly's. At Savers. They do not take pride of place at the Salvation Army any more, but they are for the picking. A dollar. Maybe fifty cents. This is not high end shopping. But they are given space in the stores, so that means someone is buying them.

But I still get stuck on the issue that hardly anyone I know can play the things. It has gone the way of the Betamax, the Super 8 home movie, photographic slides, and the passenger pigeon. So what is there to do with the VHS cassette?

I went to That's Entertainment today to look at such things as video tapes. They had a small box underneath a table laden with comic books. There was a variety of movies that most of us would not be able to watch. Rebel Rousers. The Godfather. The Day of the Daleks. The Mummy's Tomb. Gone With the Wind. Planet of the Spiders. The Hunchback of Notre Dame, The Terror. The Evil of Frankenstein. Faulty Towers. Once Upon a Time in China. Doctor Who: Robot. Hoosiers.

They are not something I can watch. But I can look at them as art. Why shouldn't we think of the covers and the back copy singing the praises of this movie as art? It is art of the hard sell. Plop your three bucks down to rent me, buddy.

I remember, when I was a kid and the land was lousy with video stores, it was sometimes more fun looking at the covers then it was to actually watch the one that was picked. I could go to the cult movie section and be amused by the cover art and the desperate tag lines. I could be holding the video tape box for Class of Nuke Em High and know that this piece of folded hard cardboard had more artistic validity then the movie it encased. Best just to hold the boxes and imagine what wonders the movie might entail. And that cinematic day dream is what good art tries to do.

I remember going into the old Starship Video on Park Avenue and just wandering and then stop and stare and wander some more. That was the same type of walk I would do in an art museum. Instead of museum guards asking me to not lean in so close, there would be annoyed cashiers wondering if I was I going to rent any movie or not.

I am sure there is someone who collects these boxes. Maybe collapse them into two dimensions and place them in mylar sleeves, to protect their value. No one can harm your mint copy of the box for Maniac Cop II.

I had a book a while back that celebrated the joy of video cassette box art. The book was The Portable Grindhouse: The Lost Art of the VHS Box. I bought it maybe ten years ago at That's Entertainment (a local epicenter for disposable art). One page was the front of a horror movie box from the eighties. Turning the page, you will see the back of the box, where all the huckster prose lingered to sell you on this one, this great horror.

I wish I could go into greater detail on the lurid joys found in that book, but I don't have it anymore. A few years after I picked it up, I found out an old school friend was sick. Tommy and I spent days and weeks and years of our youth haunting video stores looking for the best horror movies. Then we would go to one of our apartments and stay up all night watching these transvestites. We knew even then that the covers were always better than the reality when you pressed play.

When I heard of his cancer, I sent him the book with a note reminding him of all the videos we survived. He got back to me to thank me. He loved being reminded of these old movies, these old friends.

When he passed away I was unable to make it down to New York for the funeral. I don't know what happened to that book I sent him. Who knows. Things get lost. Things get donated or tossed out. All those things get in the way of moving on.

In his honor, on the day of his funeral, I stayed up through the night watching lame, awful horror movies. The only thing that was wrong with that tribute was that none of the movies were on VHS. None were wrapped in their colorful jacket of cardboard.

Four. Orphan Store Signs

I put out an eBook of a project I did during the summer of 2018. It was called Orphan Store Signs. I documented all the orphan store signs I could find throughout Worcester County. I found over a hundred and fifty of them and wrote about each of them.

What is an orphan store sign? I am so glad you asked. I think I came up with the term, though I am not quite sure. Orphan store signs are the signs to a business that is no longer. The sign is there, but the shop is closed for good or has moved or for the last three years is just closed temporarily for renovations.

I walked around Worcester and Fitchburg and Gardner and Northbridge and all the other towns with partially filled Main Street storefronts. Walking down these streets is like looking into the past. There is the Weintraub's Jewish Delicatessen sign like it is still ready to serve a bowl of matza ball soup. But it is not. Just the sign, telling little lies.

It was kind of profound walking around and making note of all these bankrupt dreams. When I started, I thought it would be a lark. I would get some good walking in and find out about all those Closed for Good shops. But as I continued through the weeks, I was taken with sadness.

I was hassled by a caretaker for a bunch of stores in Grafton. I told him I was just looking around. He said there was nothing to look at. All the places were gone and should be to. There was a flood and all the shops were deemed unsafe for occupancy. The signs still remained. Like an echo of a successful past.

I did that a year and a half ago. Now that I am writing about all these types of disposable art, my mind went to orphan store signs. The hope I kept was that many of these signs are gone and thriving businesses have taken over. This has happened with the orphan signs of the Blackstone Pub and the Canal Restaurant. Those signs have been replaced with the Rock Bar and Russo's, respectively.

So, last Monday, I decided to tool around the town and see if there are still some of the same orphan store signs from a year and a half ago.

And the sad thing is, many of them still are there. They represent nothing but the sign themselves. They are the art of remembering places we might never have gone to.

Right in downtown on Main Street in the giant yellow sign for the Great Wall Chinese Restaurant. The sign goes up several stories and is quite a sight. The restaurant has been gone for several years.

Ten feet above the street on Millbury Street is a lovely oval sign for Ciborowski Insurance Agency. I can't tell when they ended business but it has been a long time. A friend of mine has worked across the street from the sign for over a decade and has never noticed it. It's just part of the scenery we scan right over.

Still on Millbury Street we have the two signs that announce Meservey's Harding Rock Cafe. The word cafe is by itself in the larger yellow sign. There is space underneath that might be where the specials of the week were listed, or if they had a band playing the hits of the day.

I look at the sign for the Ethiopian Dream Center and wonder what amazing things happened there. Or at least, what amazing things did they try to have happen there.

When driving on 290, you can see a sign painted on a brick wall that announces the Pro-Vision Golf Performance Studio. "Learn What the Pros Know. The Numbers Simply Do Not Lie."

And let's not even talk about the yards of signage for Irish Times.

All of these signs are a reminder of hard work and bad luck. Talismans of broken hopes and scattered bands of once close co-workers. Every sign you walk under is a piece of unspoken symbolism.

On Harding Street is a beautiful sign that is also a mural and it is one of my favorite pieces of street art in all of Worcester. I think it was made for the former tattoo shop Secret Society. The word tattoo is a riot of color. There is an Illuminati eye and the words "Modern, Sterile, Electric." There are flowers and tentacles. It is an arresting piece of art and

I think it is for Secret Society. But I do not know. I am happy to see it still, but also it is too bad that it has not been replaced with new signs of current business, of new art. Art that speaks of the present.

We are always looking at the past.

Five. Beer Cans

Okay now, it's time to go to the art museum. Get ready to see a lot of art. Be prepared to be overwhelmed and thrown into shut down through sensory overload. See trends and head scratchers. That much art, you will want to scurry home and have a nice beer to calm your nerves. Well, you are in luck, because the art museum for today's field trip is at Friendly's Discount Liquor Store in Whitinsville.

Seeing art at a liquor store is a nice alternative to the expected art museum. There is no admission fee. You are allowed to touch the art, just not drink it (until purchased). You are also expected to make a stop at the gift shop (or register) and take something home. Having so much art, so much product, for you to experience, you should not be cheap and you ought to buy yourself some fine art, or at least a six pack.

When I was just a young drinker, there was not a lot of choices for beer at the store. You had the Milwaukee School of Pilsner Art and that was about it. And the cans were nothing exciting to look at or contemplate.

We are in a renaissance for beer currently. There are many small breweries, some right in town, making a wide variety of beer. And their cans and bottles are decorated with witty titles and striking visuals. Isn't it a fact that one of the side effects of the Renaissance was a focus on the arts? Well the beer can art gets that same bump.

It is like every row at the liquor store is another gallery at a museum. So much to look at. They say when you are in the market to buy fine art that you should only purchase something you are dreaming about and realize you can't live without. Isn't that the same thought process when we go and buy a half case of IPA?

Let's walk around the galleries and see what moves us. Please be quiet, or the docent who is currently removing post-date beer from the shelves, might ask us to keep it down, or they might ask for our ID. You never know.

We can start with the fine line cartoony label for Flying Dream Brewing Company's The Nightmare After Christmas. The fancy lettering informs us it is a Russian Imperial Stout.

Down a shelf and we have the good girl art of Becky Likes the Smell, a double IPA. The good girl, obviously named Becky, has a full sleeve of tattoos and is giving us a sneer.

A few beers away is a beautiful can practically radiating like a lava lamp. The beer is Charms & Hexes. There are abstract shapes that must mean something. We must stare at it longer to decipher its meaning. Art is never easy to understand.

The beer can art for Wizard Burial Ground: Bourbon Barrell Aged Quadruple Ale is like something that was airbrushed on a 1970s van. It has wizards and it is groovy.

On to another shelf we see all the different colorful cans for the Prairie Artisan Ales. These are very distinctive in name and in image. I like these very bright, cartoony cans. You see one can from this brewery and you can always identify which is theirs. It's like going into a gallery that has an exhibition of just one artist. The same is true of the shelf with the Prairie beers. The images have a Looney Tune Cartoon feel. There are characters with eyes bulging out and pumpkins checking their twitter feed. The names are great too: Apricot Funk, Bomb, Vape Tricks. It's like potable underground comix.

For more serious art, you might want to cross the aisle and check out the beer from Dieu du Ciel. They are French Canadian, so you know they got class. The labels to the bottles have a sense of dread. There is a German Expression vibe going on with this art. It is not for the faint hearted, bucko. And all the beer has French names, so that must make it important. Ah, the pretentions of art reach all the way to the beer section.

I have no idea what the beers taste of, but just looking at all these beer cans and bottle labels will make one drunk and unable to drive for at least two hours.

It is art. It gives off the art hangover just like going to a museum.

And we take the art home and we break into its top and we drink what we find inside and are very happy. But what do we do with the can? We can collect it. Put it in the basement with all the other beer cans. But no. We toss it. We are expected to. Hell, there is a deposit on all these works of art. We are not expected to keep it. Beer never lasts. That is true even for the art that wraps around it.

Six: Wheaties Boxes

In the sports section of the great collectible shop, That's Entertainment, I found a dozen Wheaties boxes for sale. Yes, for three dollars, you can take one of these bad boys home. They are all in fine shape, collapsed to form a card. There is no cereal with it. It is just the box.

Wheaties started as an accident in a lab, as most breakfast foods are. In 1921, some one spilled wheat bran mixture onto a hot stove and flakes showed up. Soon, Wheaties was for sale with that orange box. In the 1930s, the brand tied itself on to sports. It was the big name for sports and bran cereal. Eat your Wheaties. The Breakfast of Champions. Eat this and you will be the best intramural softball player that has ever been in right field.

Boxes always had a popular, successful sports figure on the box. It was a big deal to get on the Wheaties box. Now, not so much. A 2014 Washington Post article stated that Wheaties has lost 80% of market share in ten years. I don't even notice it when I walk down the cereal aisle to do my weekly shopping.

The boxes for sale at That's E seem to be from the late 90s. There is a Mark McGuire dinging 70 home runs. I think that Mark didn't eat his Wheaties to get to that number of homeruns. I think he used another type of breakfast of champions.

A few of them showed the work of Leroy Neiman. He was a very popular artist who drew painted athletes in a very distinctive, splotchy way. I remember being told how great his art was. I never bought it. Here there is a Neiman painting of Walter Paton. It looks like an athlete ran through a paint store and was smeared with samples.

That's the thing with collectable items, especially disposable items that are now told they have value, either you think they are totally cool or you wonder what the hell is wrong with the person who collected this stuff?

Older boxes of Wheaties are worth a good deal of money. And the ones from the forties and fifties have a very cool graphic quality. That's a nice way of saying, they look pretty neat.

But these newer ones. These ones are just cereal boxes without the thing that makes them worthwhile, the cereal.

Was this someone who heard that Wheaties boxes were some coin, so hoarded them, dreaming of future wealth. Oh, I know we can't pay the heating bill, but just you wait until I sell my Wheaties boxes, then we will be rolling in it.

Maybe I am being too harsh. Maybe someone loved these things. These pieces of cardboard.

Going through a memorabilia shop is an invitation to mystery. You never know what you will find. And you will never understand why someone went out of their way to save them for all these years.

It can drive a person crazy to think of it. It can make someone slightly peckish. Might I recommend a breakfast cereal? You will feel like a champion.

Seven: The Penny

I have a penny collection. I don't know where it is. It's kind of small. It was one of those little portfolios that had indentations so you can put the coins in.

The idea to this wee grouping was that I would have one penny from each year. I was going to have a century of pennies. Each penny has the year it was minted.

The other part of the collection was that all the pennies were to be found in everyday transactions. I was not to purchase from a coin dealer. I just had to get them from the change I was given, from the "leave a penny - take a penny" dishes by the cash register, on the ground, in the change jar in the kitchen.

All the pennies were to be found in the wild.

I think this little project came about when I emptied my pockets filled with, keys, coins, wadded tissues and whatever detritus nestled in there (my wife has said that I am the boy with the frog in his pocket) and discovered a few old pennies. One was from the seventies. Another was 1969. Then I noticed a penny from 1946.

I was shocked. There was a lot of hard living right there resting in my palm So, for a few years, I was determined to get a penny from every year. I think the earliest penny I got was from the 1920s.

It was amazing to see how the humble penny had changed. From heavy dark metal of the 1940s to the shiny pliable penny of 2002. The older ones seemed more valuable. Though, point of fact, they still were just a cent.

I never finished the collection. Hell, I don't even know where they are. I hope I didn't sacrifice them to the false god of CoinStar, one of those days I was feeling poor and thrifty. I think it's been a decade since I found a coin that could be added to the collection.

But I think of those stout little guys often. I can hold a penny from 1943 pinched between my fingers and wonder on the long history it has had.

Did kids gamble with it, pitching it up against the wall?

Was it thrown into a cup to help the war effort?

Was it collected with other like-minded coins so that the ragged man can get a room, with a clean bed, for the night?

Was it pin money for a housewife?

Was it thrown up and the air as someone shouted "heads.

Was it picked up lucky?

How many comic books did it help purchase?

How many times was it used to buy some penny candy?

How many times was it thrown into a dirty coffee cup sitting in front of a bearded man holding a cardboard sign asking for change?

How many pairs of penny loafers was it a part of?

All of these coins have a long life. They are worn and beautiful. This century of pennies has a long story to tell us.

This penny has a history that is rich and valuable. And it is worth, almost, nothing.

Update: This column is a little bothersome for me. It was based on an old performance poem I used to do. I changed it enough to feel like I was creating something new. But in the time I wrote it to when it was published, six months had passed. In that time, I was introduced to a terrific singer-songwriter, Guy Clark. He is worth discovering. While I was getting into his catalog, I listened to his song, "Indian Head Penny." That song does the same thing I do in the column, only better. It is awesome. I planned to tell Victor not to use this column, but then I found out that it was already published. Oh well. So, read this column and then listen to Clark's song. You can compare and contrast the two. Write two to three pages, make sure you double space. - David

Eight: T-Shirt

It was one of those weeks where I probably should have done a few large loads of laundry, because the shelves were getting a little thin on clean clothes. I reached up and pulled out one of the few remaining t-shirts. It was a plain tee, a nice golden rod yellow. I didn't know I had a plain tee of this color, but that was fine. I put it on and went about my day.

It was a few hours later that I noticed something was off with the shirt. It seemed that I got something smudged on it. This is not a rare occurrence. I am a sloppy eater. Food stains on my shirt is just an indication that I liked the meal. On closer inspection, I realized that it wasn't a smudge, but a faded image. I looked hard at it and saw the faint black ink image of a ladybug.

A ladybug! I remember this t-shirt.

We had gone to an art gallery up in Portsmouth. There was some cool prints done with linotype (I don't know what that is, just saying) of animals but done in an 8 Bit retro video game style. In addition to the prints, the artist put some of the images on t-shirts. I bought the ladybug shirt for something like twenty dollars.

The question is, was it just a shirt or was I wearing art? I suppose that for the most part it was something to wear, but I liked the image, I liked the memory of the time in the gallery. I guess it was both things.

But there is an issue if you are washing your art every few weeks after wear. If I wore that shirt 25 times, then it was thrown into the washer that many times.

I guess it was fading from the minute I got it. It stayed in the closet for some time and then it was out the other day and the image is just a ghost. A shadow. No one knows, but me, that hidden in the spaces in the cloth is a cool piece of art. Everyone else will think it is a dirty shirt and I should know better to wear it. It's not a smudge! It's art!

I also have a t-shirt where Tom Waits used to cavort. I picked the shirt up at a Record Store Day seven years ago. It was a gray shirt with a strong graphic of Tom Waits and guitar leaping in front of a stack of amps. You can tell this was a favorite shirt because it has been washed to a tabula rasa. There are dark, unfocused things on the shirt. I know what they are. I still love the image; the image that I can hardly make out. It is a gallery for one.

There are a lot of broken canvases in my shirt shelf. There are the shirts with busted seems that I can't wear but I cannot bear to toss them out. The shirts so faded no one knows what once was on the front. The shirts that don't fit because time and age shrinks them (I will say that instead of the fact that I ain't the beanpole I once was.)

But this is private. T-Shirts are a portal to a time and place. They are so dear that no one will understand your devotion to it. It isn't what the shirt is, it is what happened when it was worn.

This column was written in the dining room, wearing a 19 year old t-shirt. I got it as part of a wedding party. I was honored to be the best man. I got this light gray shirt with a graphic design of a sailboat on the back. It is nothing special. It is very thin in spots. I love it to pieces. And I am sure that when it is in pieces, I will treasure it all the more.

Update: *This was aided by the assistance of my old friend Foster. He shows up in another article, giving me good advice.* I still wear those two t-shirt. I wore the Tom Waits shirt yesterday and got a few hard stares. Was there an image on the shirt? What the hell am I seeing?

Nine: The Shredded

Here is the thing with disposable art, sometimes it is disposable not because it isn't wonderful to look at and hold, but because the creator thinks that it should be destroyed. He makes it disposable.

In Franz Kafka's last will, he asked for his work be destroyed. All of his stories, his unfinished novels, were to be destroyed. I am sure there are some out there who were forced to read his work in school who wished that it did happen. But the man who was supposed to destroy the work upon Kafka's death, Max Brod, didn't. We are allowed to experience the work because of a bad friend breaking his word. Thank god.

A few years back a woman won a Banksy painting at an auction at Sotheby's. She paid 1.4 million dollars for the painting, Girl with Balloon. As soon as she won it and purchased it, Banksy's people activated a device in the painting's frame and the painting went down into the frame and was shredded. It was a prank to protest the moneyed world of art. I guess.

Don't think of it as a destruction of art but a transformation. The buyer kept the remains of the frame and the painting. Banksy renamed it as Love is in the Bin.

I know of many people who loved what Banksy did, but I am not too keen on the stunt. Because money still passed hands. He still got over a million dollars for the art. And the painting that the customer bid on and won, was destroyed. What was intended to be given for money was not.

I like the idea of destroying the art you make. I like the transitory. The ephemeral. It's when money is involved that it gets muddy and unpleasant.

The purest version of this, in my opinion, was by a local poet Tony Brown. Around twenty years ago he had a feature at the Java Hut. But he prepared for it differently than other poetry features he did.

He wrote brand new poems for the feature. He wrote them on the computer, printed them out, and then deleted the computer file. So the only copy of the poem was the print out. He did that for all these poems.

When he began, he asked for a volunteer. The way it then worked was that Tony read the poem and when it was one, it was given to the volunteer. The volunteer then had to tear it up into pieces. The poem is read, and then all evidence of the poem is destroyed.

I wasn't there. I missed it. Actually, Tony has done this type of feature a few more times and I missed each one. That first one is pretty legendary. People still talk of it. I heard the volunteer who had to rip up the pages was upset. Someone else built a little plexiglass container of the ripped up pages. I know of other poets have performed this way as well.

The poetry is just for that one moment. It is read and it cannot be read again. You might remember a line that was amazing, but after a while, you might remember it wrong. The poem changes in memory.

The art is not disposable. The way the poem makes you feel and think is not disposable. But it is created to not last.

I like this so much more than what Banksy did, because this didn't have a million dollar price tag to it. This was about one instance where an artist shared with an audience for that one specific moment in time. Who says art needs to hang around? Who needs it more than once? If the work is good, powerful and true, it only needs one time to change a person.

Ten: Cardboard Records

You know I am so much cooler than all these hipsters who have discovered old records like they made them themselves. And how they all talk about vinyl. "I'm into vinyl." Or "The Music sounds truer when it's on vinyl."

Me? I don't go for that kind of record. Who needs something so common as vinyl? Me, I go for cardboard records.

What are cardboard records, I hear you cry? They are exactly what it sounds like. They were pieces of cardboard you played on your record player. They were coated with a thin plastic that had the grooves needed to make the music.

They sounded like shit. How could they not, they were made of cardboard. They came in magazines. They came as a premium at McDonald's. But for me, they came on the back of a cereal box.

On the back of specially marked boxes of Rice Krispies, there would be a section that you could cut out and like that, you have a cardboard record. And not just any record, but cardboard records with songs by everyone's favorite rock sensation, the Archies.

Oh, I guess I now have to explain the disposable art of the Archies. The Archies was a band with many hits like Sugary Sugar. Actually, the Archies were never a band. They were session musicians who threw together a bunch of bubblegum pop songs that played on the Archie cartoon show on Saturday Mornings. Archie and his band would play a song at the end of the cartoon and we would hear one of these songs made for the show.

There was a weird tradition in the cartoons of the sixties and seventies, that there should be new rocking music for the cartoons. It is an amazing concept, "Let's make disposable music for the disposable Saturday morning cartoon." It's like a puzzle box with wheels upon wheels.

The weird thing is, even though the Archies songs were never meant to be anything other than something in a cartoon, it made it to the radio. They played on America's Top Forty. Their songs were huge. I love the fakeness of the Archies. Who needs autotune when you have the cartoon redhead having a top ten hit.

But they were not the only band that had cardboard record success. On the back of Alphabits and Super Sugar Crisp cereals, you could get one of five Jackson Five records. The Jackson Five were huge, they were live people who became Saturday morning cartoons.

The amazing aspect to the whole cardboard record was that you had to cut it from the cereal box yourself. You had to cut out your own entertainment. You had to free it. Cut that out yourself. Kids these days, now you download all the music you want on your phone in just a few seconds while in my day, we had to cut our music our of the back of a Rice Krispies cereal box.

I remember cutting a few of these from the box and it was there that my deficit of cutting was evident. I have a memory of cutting one of the records too closely. I cut out the first thirty seconds of the song. Knowing the songs they used, I don't think I missed anything. But that does stress the fact that every cardboard record is a unique, one-of-a-kind objects d'art. Made from little hands, you can see the jagged cut lines represent man's struggle against nature.

Those records, which were on many a cereal box, did not last. Why didn't it survive? Well they were made of cardboard. They were not made to last. And they were given to kids and kids can never hold onto anything. And a lot of people got rid of all their records when that new thing the CD player came along and told us that any older technology is useless. Why would they hold onto something made of cardboard that played only two minutes of song when you weren't keeping all those full LPs?

It is the perfect piece of disposable art. They were cut, played once and then forgotten.

But I can't help but think of the kid who was raised with very little. She had nothing much of her own. I see her visiting her aunt and having a bowl of Rice Krispies and the aunt letting her cut out the record from the back of the box. There she is, walking home proudly, with the first music record that is hers and hers alone. I can see her playing that Archies record on her father's beat up record player until there is no more music left on the flimsy disc. The music is in her. Her first record. Her first song that was hers and hers alone.

When I see these pieces of cut up cardboard, I must think of the one who found it precious.

Update: *We got some reader response to this one. The writer remembered his favorite record, which was a flexi-disc that was included in an issue of Mad Magazine. The song was "She Got a Nose Job." I found it on YouTube and listened to it. And I am here to say, I survived. It was a tough go. Now, the funny part is that, if I was a kid, I would have thought this was the funniest damned thing I ever heard.*

Eleven: Autographed Copies

The recent passing of David Prowse, the actor who played Darth Vader in the first three Star Wars films, made me remember the one time I met him.

I was ten years old. It was 1979. I was visiting family in New York City. My Uncle, realizing that I loved comic books to an insane degree, took me to a new kind of store. It was a comic book shop. Who knew that such delights were even legal?

The shop was situated in the Upper East Side. It had the odd luck of being named Super Snipe. They took the name from an obscure 1940s comic book. Of course, when you looked at it, most comics were obscure

The shop was really small. You had to wait outside for others to leave. It could only fit ten customers at a time. When we did get in, I was in some higher plane of existence. A store dedicated to nothing but comic books. It was sublime.

It took me a few minutes to focus enough to see comics that I wanted. There was the first issue of the new series of Man-Thing. It was about a sentient swamp monster and I had to have it. I clutched it to my chest, afraid that someone would take it from me.

Suddenly, the door to the store opened and a giant strode in. It was amazing he could fit in the shop. A much smaller man ran like a terrier behind him and shouted, "David Prowse, Darth Vader himself is here and he will sign your Star Wars comics."

The giant of a man spoke to someone thrusting a comic at him. He had a lilting Scottish accent. I was bewildered, I saw Star Wars ten times, and that was not Darth Vader's voice. My uncle explained that David Prowse was in the costume and another actor, James Earl Jones, was the voice. I was dubious, but I had to give my uncle the benefit of the doubt. He had, after all, taken me to a comic shop.

There was little room to avoid this huge celebrity. Soon, I was before him. He was six foot six. I was four foot something. I only came up to his abdomen. He was like a fairy tale creature. In that sweet, tenor voice he said to me, "You want me to sign your comic?"

Sure. I thrust in front of him my copy of Man-Thing #1. He opened it up and began to sign his name. He only made it to the letter "D" before his handler angrily said, "He's not going to sign that comic. Buy a Star Wars comic, he'll sign that." David Prowse nodded sadly from way up in the stratosphere.

Someone put into my hands a copy of Star Wars #29. It had a great cover of Darth Vader fighting a cyborg. Mr. Prowse took it and signed the first page. I believe he wrote, "David Prowse is Darth Vader."

He gave it back to me and now I had a comic I really didn't want, but it was signed by Darth Vader, so that must have been good. After only a few minutes, Darth Vader and his handler had left the building and we all were able to breathe again.

I love recalling that moment with David Prowse. This was before celebrities such as he would make a lot of money signing things. All I had to do was buy a forty cent Star Wars comic. Maybe that was the real worth of someone's signature back then.

Signatures are big time collectables. But all they are, are a name. An affirmation of identity. We force the value on it. We make it significant by sheer will.

Over the years, my comic book collection got to be immense. I sold it off a long time ago and I no longer have that signed Star Wars comic.

But the comic I probably miss more is that Man-Thing #1 with the letter "D" sprawled on the first page. Somewhere in the world, someone owns that copy of the book and am sure is annoyed that a crazy kid wrote on the first page, destroying the value. They don't know who graffitied on their book. Would they be impressed that Darth Vader wrote that letter "D"? Or would they still want it to be pristine and unblemished?

Update: My sister wanted to remind me that she was also at Super Snipe that day and also met the giant that was David Prowse. I have no idea how I could ever have omitted my sister's existence when telling a cool story. How could I do such a thing?

Twelve: Candy Necklace

I'm sure this happens to you all the time. You are sitting around, doing nothing, making no mischief, when in pops a notion into your head, "What is the history of the candy necklace? And why are people not wearing them around to put a little sweetness into their bling?" Yes. We all have such thoughts, there is nothing to be ashamed to think such things.

Has anyone spent time, I mean serious time, wearing a chandy necklace or the smaller, candy bracelet? Have you sashayed your way home with a few ounces of candy wrapped around your neck?

My son tells me of a kid at his school who would start the day with five candy bracelets on his wrist. He ate about a bracelet an hour. At the end of the day, he would be without candy bracelets and he also then spoke in a tongue that no one could understand.

No one knows the real origin of the candy bracelet. Some things of greatness are shrouded in mystery. One place said there was a rumor that they came from Northern Europe. I love the word they used, rumor. Like people, at candy conferences, whisper what their grandparents told them about a world in the frozen North where not only did people eat candy, but they wore it too.

What we do know for certain is that in the late fifties the candy necklace was introduced. They tend to use the Smarties candy.

I have to ask, who thought that candy worn around a kid's neck was a good idea? A kid who has been running around the neighborhood this entire humid day. And now that he needs a break, he will eat pieces of his necklace, for energy. There is nothing more delicious than a candy coated in neck sweat. Yum-yum.

I suppose it is either a candy dirty from sweat or the candy left alone on the kid's pocket, gathering up all the lint and tissue paper it can around its body. Wow. It just occurred to me. I am shocked about what our parents let us eat as kids.

The problem with candy necklaces as disposable art is that it really is not that artistic. It's just a string of sucking candies around a child's neck. It does not cry out, "This is art that was not meant to last!" The only thing it says to me when I see one around a fifth grader is, "Oh man, that kid is gonna be off the wall all afternoon!"

I am disappointed to not find any beautiful diamond rings made from the finest of hard candies. I guess they are out there, but I can't find them.

What I have found is candy turning into jewelry, not the other way around. There are a few jewelers who take candy and encase it in resin. They then put the resined candy on necklaces or earrings or rings. You want licorice candy earrings or a Jordan almond necklace? That can happen. With real candy, but you can't eat it. It will last for years. It can be a heirloom handed down from daughter to daughter. "I am giving you your grandmother's favorite piece of jewelry, the tennis bracelet made from gummy bears. I know she will be smiling down when you wear it."

This would not fit as disposable art. This is art that uses candy as a starting block. I pity the candy starved fool who tries to bite into the Jordan Almond ring.

I guess what I would like to see is someone wearing a candy necklace and not eating it away until it is only naked elastic. They could eat it, they could make it go away, but chose not to. They like the way it looks on them. They like that pop of pastel color around their neck. They are not saving the dessert for later, but making a fashion statement for the here and now.

And when your friends see that you are no longer sporting such a fine piece of jewelry around your neck, you can tell them, "I needed a change of style. And besides, I got hungry."

Thirteen: Video Game Music

Sitting down in the office to write this, my son came to join in, writing his own things. He took out a record and put it on the stereo. It is the soundtrack to Battlefield V. It is a lush orchestral piece of music. It is sad and monumental, at turns. And it was written for a video game. My son has been introduced to so many different kinds of music because of video games. He found a love of 40s harmony groups, such as the Ink Spots, from playing Fallout. He discovered Willie Nelson through Red Dead Redemption 2. And the Battlefield games have a large cinemascope type soundtrack.

This should not be a big surprise. Video game music is a big thing. A lot of musicians make some living wages from putting out music for the latest first person shooter. Scott Campbell, the founder of Post Modern Jukebox, made his first splash by making music for a Biohazard game. Large philharmonic orchestras have their most financially successful concerts when they program video game music. How are people introduced to music now? Through the music they hear every day, shooting em up, rescuing the princess. That kind of thing.

I am old. To me the music of video games were the plink-plink-plink of the ball hitting the paddle on a game of Pong. Or the pwew-pwew shooting sounds in Galaga. The only way to hear such a melody was to put a quarter in the game and play your three lives. It was like listening to songs on a jukebox. I know, what the hell is a jukebox?

For me, the most iconic music from video games has to be from Super Mario Brothers. And the amazing thing about that music, is that the composer, Koji Kondo was quite limited by the amount of space he had for the pre-recorded sound. He could not go crazy with what he could do. So with such limitations, comes a melody we all know and love. Do we love it because of the ingenuity or in spite of it?

If you want to go down a rabbit hole, or a drain pipe because we are talking about Mario Brothers, then go to YouTube and put in a Super

Mario Brothers theme cover. There are a lot of choices. My favorite at the moment is the Post Modern Jukebox (them again) where they do it with a Dixey Land combo and a tap dancer. Got to have a tap dancer for your video game music covers!

There are books that analyze the music from that first Super Mario Brothers book. The books explain that the music is there to create a mood. It allows you to know what is coming. If the music speeds up, then you better speed the hell up too, because you are running out of time to clear that world. Different music tells you that there are new expectations.

The music was there to inform the player about certain things. And also, it needed to swing baby!

Kondo, who has done tons of great music for games, has been interviewed endlessly about the original Super Mario Brothers music. In one of the interviews, he said, "music is inspired by the game controls, and its purpose is to heighten the feeling of how the game controls." I love that. The music was a teaching tool to start to understand how to play the game better. It was not meant to be covered by countless performers on YouTube. Its purpose was to help you get to the Princess with efficiency. To win the game. To save the day.

A few years ago, we took the kid to Fun Spot in Laconia, New Hampshire. It has something like 300 vintage video games. That's a lot of sound. That's a lot of 8 Bit Music playing at once. When we walked in, it was like the sound of all that composition playing at once would knock us over. It was a riot of music and sound designed to entice you to play this one and not that one. It was there to help you learn when to jump, when to shoot, when to run away fast. There was no way to hear any one game. It was a whirlwind of sampling and explosions. The only way to hear one song was to lean into your chosen game and get as close to the action as possible. You had to give yourself up to the game to hear the song. A song of play and conflict and rebirth (usually three lives per quarter.) An earworm. You will be singing that tiny tinny melody for the rest of the day. Or even longer.

Fourteen: Decorative Hand Soap

Okay. Soap that you are not allowed to use. It was a thing. Most of the time, they were in the shape of a shell. They were in the bathroom. They were probably below a nicely folded hand towel, that you were also not supposed to touch.

In most tellings of this, it's the grandmother who has the bowl of decorative soap. And do not piss off grandma. I wouldn't even look at those soaps. You have been warned.

I have a lot of questions about this. The first being, why should there be soap that is not allowed to be used? It's soap! The very definition of the thing means that you touch it. In this new age of social distancing and constant handwashing, we see a piece of soap, we expect to use it. But you put it in the form of a shell and it's a huge, do not enter sign flashing.

The next question I have is, why seashells? It's almost always soap in the shape of the discarded hard outer layer of a sea creature. The real shells are created by the animals. The soap shells were made from a mold in a factory. What makes the facsimile of a seashell such an important artifact?

My last question has to be, why did all the grandmothers protect these pieces of cleaning material like they were masterpieces on loan from the Louvre?

To see if I might get some answers to these questions, I put them all to the Board of Directors of the Library of Disposable Art (a venerable crowd). They responded that they too had experience with the Verboten Soap!

Jeff Campbell tells us, "My mom had these translucent bars... they had like shells or stones or something in them? She was this incredibly kind, loving and compassionate woman. And she utterly lost her shit when my young cousin clawed them, used them to wash his hands." Paul

McMahon clarifies what types of soap he was dealing with, " Mostly shaped like scallop shells and shark eye shells. Maybe even a starfish one."

Christine Guest tells an almost optimistic tale, "My grandma had a pair that looked like cameos. One had Martha Washington's face, the other George. I think they were bi-centennial things? I did wash my hands with Martha, but Grandma was gracious about it." A gracious grandma dealing with matters of the decorative soap? Not in my neighborhood!

The part I really don't get is that even though we are not allowed to use the soap, it is always placed right there in the bathroom, inches from the sink. It's like it is mocking us.

The always philosophical Deb Middleton was able to shine some light when she wrote, " It was something you just had to have to have the proper, respectable home. It was also a status symbol, you had enough money to have something decorative like that, even if you didn't, it made people think you did." Well, that definitely answers some of the questions. It was an affordable way to look classy. And if it is losing definition because the soap is being used, then it ain't classy no more.

The other name I came across for this item was Guest Soap. This was the good soap for the good people who might visit. The kids are not good. Let them use ugly, ordinary soap. The kind of soap we are ashamed of.

Decorative soap is a perfect candidate for the Library of Disposable Art. If the soap is used correctly, then it should be worn down to nothing. It should keep your hands clean, not be pleasing to the eye and nose (because a lot of these little darlings were scented). Soap, in whatever shape it may be in, is meant to lather and shrink. Soap is a functional tool. It should not be encased in plastic, like the furniture in your aunt's front room.

There are still mysteries to this phenomena. Mostly, why shells? Really. Why is the motif always seashells? Stuff like that keeps me up at night.

But this is an issue that seems to be fading. All the people who responded to my queries are middle aged. We are remembering our grandmothers doing this. But what of our children? They probably were not exposed to such prohibitions, because we wouldn't do it to them. We let our kids use the soap, because dammit, it's soap. We will not subject them to this because we still have the scars. It makes us feel all dirty. Like we need to wash up. With whatever piece of soap is at hand.

Fifteen: Collectible Glasses

The other day, I noticed one of our Star Wars glasses sitting on the coffee table, minding its own business, I am sure. I picked it up and brought it over to the sink. I placed it down in the sink, with a vague plan of washing it sometime that evening. I didn't get the chance. The act of placing it in the sink caused it to lose its will to be whole. It broke into five large pieces. I slowly fished them out and threw them away.

Now you should know, they aren't just any Star Wars glasses you can pick up at Target. No, sir. Not for us. No, we are too cool for Target pop culture detritus. No, these were vintage glasses given as a promotion for the Return of the Jedi. They are from a long time ago, 1983. That makes them 37 years old. They were given out with an order of Coke at Burger King.

There were five or six different Return of the Jedi glasses, collect them all if you dare. They have wrap around illustrations of scenes from the movie. There are Ewoks and C3PO. There is the glass about Han Solo on the Moon of Endor. And there is the one with Jabba the Hutt on the Sand Barge. (For those of you not Star Wars fans, you are reading this wondering what off market drugs I might be taking, but be reassured, that all of this makes serious sense, for those in the know) It was a premium. If you bought a certain type of drink, you got the glass. You might have to pay a little more for the glass, but why wouldn't you? You are getting a delicious Whopper and a great Star Wars glass. You should buy extra. Who knows. They might be valuable years from now.

I think I bought one of these glasses for the first time at That's Entertainment, the great comic and weirdness shop in the city. My son, who was eight at the time, thought it was the greatest thing in the world. He felt that chocolate milk tasted better in the glass. Who am I to disagree with such a reasoned opinion?

But it was made of glass. Glass feels good when you drink from it. Glass also breaks. It wasn't too long before we had no Star Wars: Empire Strikes Back Burger King Glass. My son was upset. He was in tears.

Father to the rescue. I went on eBay and bought a set of six of the glasses. They came two weeks later with two of the glasses broken. So we had four.

This has been the history of these glasses. We buy them on eBay and one by one they shatter into history. This is how it has gone for years.

So, the other day one of the glasses of the latest set broke and I told my son and reminded him that we had two left. He was upset. I wasn't expecting it. He is twelve now and I figured maybe there wouldn't be such an attachment to 40 year old fast food restaurant premiums. "I like having them. My favorite ones always break first." Father to the rescue.

And over the years, the damned glasses are getting more expensive on eBay. This stands to reason because as the years pass we all break these things and they become slightly more scarce. There are still a lot of them out there, but gone are the days I could get a full set for twelve bucks.

I like them. I drink from an Ewoks glass or a Jabba the Hutt glass almost every day. My son does not. These are not the glasses he is looking for. He likes looking at them. He likes our act of possession. But he just would rather drink from a wider glass.

Soon, we will break so many of them that they will become too valuable to drink from. They will have to be kept away from the vagaries of finger muscles and stress fractures. They will be kept in a cabinet used solely for their safety. They will be kept under glass.

And to think, these were pieces of promotion. They said "Collect Them All" and wanted you to buy them. No one expected them to change into some worthy. They would things that would be kept and preserved and cried over when all that remains are shards.

Sixteen: The Pet's in the Mail

When I was a kid, I think one of the best parts about the comics I picked up at the drug store were the ads. I was fascinated about the full page ads for the Sea Monkeys. I never bought them, because I didn't want my mail order animals to have human-like faces. If I was to judge from what I would get from the picture, I was going to get small human-like creatures, and I just didn't think I could handle that.

There were also all the ads to teach me how to be big and muscled. I was no longer going to have sand kicked in my face, even if I was cool about it. Or I could not just be buff, but have the martial arts skills to kill a man with a viper technique. This sounded like a good investment of my five dollars.

Recently, I have dived back into these old mags and I linger on these weird little ads. There was one that made me take pause. It was a small one, only a few inches in size, but gigantic in imagination.

It read. "Baby Raccoons! One of America's Favorite Pets! Has always been and still is. Easy to care for. $29.95 with cage. Send cashier's check or money order along with your phone number and nearest airport. Hialeah Pets. Department 35. Hialeah, Florida."

America's favorite pet? Really? In what America? And the idea that these are baby raccoons and not full grown ones. As if they will never grow up. They are Peter Pan raccoons. The lost boys of scavenger animals. And don't you think your mother will be so excited for you to have a pet at last?

In my house growing up, we were not allowed pets. We could have hamsters and gerbils, but they hardly count as pets. They are more ornaments with wood chips.

The part that gets me the most is that there are at least 34 other departments at this most reputable of mail order pet purveyors. From another ad I saw online, there is a department 16 where the monkeys are purchased. I wonder what other impractical pets are behind the other numbers. What a joy. What a natural disaster.

I was able to find online a story by a guy who claims that he saved his money and ordered a monkey from one of these ads. He was able to get someone to pick it up at the airport. And when he got the monkey out of the cage, it immediately tore the kid's face up. Can you blame it? The family kept the monkey, but it did not live long.

For me, I think these ads are important not for getting a wild animal through the mail, but just to imagine what joy it would be to own a monkey or a baby raccoon. The price was high for a kid back then, so all we could do was dream. "All the kids will see me with my monkey on a leash and think I am so cool."

The quality of the daydream is up to how much you can believe. The ads in the old comics were fantasy. Things we can create in our heads. What a joy. What a natural disaster.

Seventeen: Scented Candles

When I was a young man, I lived in Hyannis in Cape Cod. We got an apartment close to downtown, which was great. The rent was cheap. Probably because it was two miles from the Cape Cod airport and planes were constantly flying overhead. And another reason is that we were a block away from the Colonial Candle Factory. At all hours of the day, a toxic cloud of mixed votive scents invaded the neighborhood. If we were stumbling home after a night of sampling the Hyannis bars, we were immediately sobered up through the boot camp version of aromatherapy that was passing the candle factory. All traces of alcohol fled from the one two combo punch of vanilla and patchouli. We would inhale when we reached the block and exhaled only after passing the factory.

That might be why I just don't understand the scented candle scene. Some of the candles smell nice, but then you have to remember to burn them safely. And sometimes what smelled nice in the store now feels like it's stinking up your home. For some people, they love using the scented candles. For others, they just don't understand why they were given it as a present by a distant cousin. Do I look like a candle person?

My wife gave me a Father's Day gift of a candle that had the scent of pipe smoke. Now, I don't smoke. But I have admitted to my wife that one of my fondest memories of my father is the pipe always dangling out of his mouth, and the persistent odor of the sweet tobacco wherever he had been. That's a fine present. I am happy I got it. Now, I don't ever plan to light it, because we don't use candles in the house. And even though the odor brings back many memories, do I want the house smelling of it? Nostalgia is a wonderful thing, but do you want the house stinking of it?

A few years ago, a company put out a five candle mini-votive set in honor of Star Wars: A New Hope. Each candle had a different and distinct odor. You had five iconic aspects of the film masterpiece enshrined in scent. There was: Bantha Milk, Wookie, X-Wing Cockpit, Trash Compactor and Canteen. Those are some all over the place scents.

A review commented that none of the scents were awful, but none were particularly pleasing either. Say what you will about a candle set that has Trash Compactor as a scent, the set sold out quickly.

But the question I have for those that bought for it themselves or for their dear friends, did anyone plan on using them as candles? This was something witty and fun to show to friends when they came over. They will ask, "Have you used them?" and you will reply, "Are you crazy?" A conversation starter more than anything else. That set has value because no one would ever use it for its intended purpose.

Candles are an odd creature. It makes light. The flame itself is beautiful, you can be lost in the flicker and fade that you stare at in the center of the flame. The candle also can be gorgeously constructed. They are pieces of sculpture art and there are many candles that will never be burned. They are just pretty as is. Like the decorative soaps and the fancy hand towels that grandma insists never to be used, there is a breed of candle that is lit at your own risk.

Scented candles are slightly different. They usually are not pretty looking. They are supposed to smell pretty, or soothing. Some people use them. Some people keep them in their bathroom closet, because his sister in-law insists on giving them as gifts. Is she trying to say the house stinks?

But even if you use five scents at once and the place smells confused, the odor will pass. It will not last. Like the candle burning at both ends, it doesn't stick around. Like all things of disposable art, it stays on as a memory. Hey, you remember when the apartment smelled of rose hips? Or, the fact that that smell of pipe brings my father back for a brief second, like a quick flicker of a candle flame?

Eighteen: Toys in the Box

One of the first fights my wife and I ever had was when she moved in with me and we unpacked her Charlie Brown toy figures. She had a lot of them. Snoopy and Woodstock. There was Lucy and Linus dressed for Halloween. (I got a rock.) The little action figures were still in the original packaging. "Why don't you take them out so you can pose them and play with them?" She gave me a steely look and I had the sensation that I said something VERY bad. She informed me that taking them out of the package was a deal break for the relationship. They came in the original packaging and they were going to stay that way.

But this is not about me. This is about the refusal of many adults to take their toys out of the package. There is a whole generation of toy creatures that will be forever encased in original plastic.

You know what is better than having a Boba Fett action figure? Having a Boba Fett action figure that has never been taken out of the package. Or a Donatello Ninja Turtle doll. That thing better be in its plastic card for it to be worthy of collecting.

This has been a thing for decades with toy collectors. Toys in the original box are better than the toys themselves. We want things to be pristine. We want things to be untouched by human hands.

But the things that are untouched by human hands, were meant to be played with by kids. I know we are adults and are wrapped with mortality and nostalgia. We want the toys of our youth. We begin to collect Star Wars or Ninja Turtles or Transformers. And to really make it perfect. Not only do we plan to never play with the toy we spent so much money on, we demand that no one else ever touched it as well. We want our toys to be like cloistered nuns.

What you will have is a piece of plastic encased in plastic. You will have an object d'art and not a toy. You will have a facsimile of a toy.

I know that I am annoying all the toy collectors out there, but I will say it. Screw the resale value. Take the toys out and have some fun. You know, fun. Like playing with the toys you loved when you were a kid.

Display your GI Joe toys in odd poses. Let them cavort with the Barbie dolls that you also released from their plastic prison. Put them in dioramas. Perch them on the edge of bookshelves. Take them out in the wild and take action photographs with them. Hold on to that doll you always wanted when you were a kid, and whisper small truths into its plastic ear.

That Meco Spider Man action figure from 1975 is dying in his box. He can't breathe. He is suffocating. He has been stuck in that box for 46 years. Imprisoned with no trial. No crime. He is the victim of the insidious penal system and the toy market. Release him now. The DNA evidence has come back inconclusive. Free the Holly Hobby Seven!

I don't understand the appeal of a toy that has never been played with. It doesn't feel like a thing of great value. It feels like the saddest creation in the world.

Nineteen: Miniature Liquor Bottles

Last time I was in Vermont, I went into a junk shop. Here is a question, when did we stop calling stores with an accumulation of stuff, junk shops? Now they are antique malls. Or vintage emporiums. When did we stop calling them junk shops? Now, I am not denigrating the things found in such places. I mean, some of my best friends are junk.

Whatever you need to call it, this place was a packed and over teeming cornucopia of junk, and I loved it. I was wandering about, with no intention to buy anything. My wife really is done with me buying useless things to clutter the house with. She says, I clutter the house well enough just by my very presence. No need to bring anything else into the mix.

But then, near the register, there was a large box that said, "Old bottles. One dollar each." These were not just old bottles. They were miniature old bottles. They were miniature old liquor bottles.

You know. Nips. Those shrunken vessels found in hotel mini-bars and in the rolling beverage carts of airplanes. Or you might find them stuffed inside a pinata. (This is true. A friend told me that for her partner's 30th birthday, they had a pinata filled with nips. Though that was not a great idea what with them being hit with a bat and then falling on the ground, they did tend to break all over the place.)

I rummaged through the box and found the three most interesting shaped bottles. The guy at the counter was amused I was buying them. "You know, some of them still have some of their booze in them." As if this was an enticing selling point.

I just smiled at him and handed over my three bucks. I couldn't explain to him that these three old bottles were wonderful examples of disposable art. Nothing is more disposable than a nip bottle. They are not meant to hang about. They are to be carried in a pocket and quickly consumed and then tossed away.

Next time you walk through the neighborhood, look down at the gutter and you will see nips tossed here, there and the next place. Conceptual art of the quick buzz. The stratification of thirst shrunk down to its smallest dividend.

I can't conceive of anyone keeping these bottles. Each one is at least twenty five years old. Why would anyone keep them? But someone did. Looking on eBay, I found that some of these bottles are for sale for over ten dollars. No one is saying that the seller will get such a fortune, but they are trying.

They are dirty things, this trio. In the bottle of Guest House Port Wine there is a dark purple crust on the bottom from the dried wine. The Sabra Chocolate Orange Liquor bottle (a fine Isreali product, that is now no longer made in Israel) also has the dried remnants of its elixir caked on the inside of the bottle. Someone didn't drink every drop.

It is impossible to clean them. If you wash them out, you will ruin the paper label. So you are stuck with a dusty old bottle with a few drops of bad port wine. (That friend who had the Nip Pinata was shocked that I was not going to taste the few remaining drops of port wine. She felt I was a poor columnist for not tasting what I am writing about. Well, anyone who has ever read this column knows what a poor columnist I am, so why ruin my taste buds?)

I bought the last ancient nip bottle for its name. Camus Cognac. I do love a bottle of booze named after 20th Century French Existentialists. If you need to understand the Myth of Sisyphus, just have a few sips of this, and it will all make sense.

We are pack rats. We keep everything. We even keep the glass that held the booze we drank too quickly the night before. Hangovers are transitory. The glass that gave us that pain can stay with us as long as we have shelf space.

I picked the bottles because they were a nice shape. According to my research, the Sabra bottle is based on an ancient Phoenician decanter. See. Fancy. The Guest House Port Wine is three sided. Two of the sides have indentations, probably to aide in tipping that bad boy back and having the drink slide right down the throat.

My wife saw them and mused that they looked like perfume bottles. I am sure there were many people given scent from these bottles.

Looking at them on a shelf, what joy of art will you find? What absence will you feel?

Twenty: Tea Box Menagerie

I don't know why I was ignorant about these critters, but I had no idea about the Red Rose Tea Figurines. My family drank Lipton Tea. We were not Red Rose folk. When I asked some people in the Library Braintrust what I should write about next, several of them mentioned the Red Rose Animals.

Red Rose Animals?

I asked my wife about them. "Did you know that there are little animals in the boxes of tea? I guess it's a thing."

My wife gave me one of those exasperated, husbands are the dumbest creatures looks, stared at my sorry face and said, "We have them all over the house. My grandma loved them. I keep them for her. I mean I have some right there." She pointed to a bookcase, and right on top was a tiny ceramic polar bear. There was a bison. There was a capuchin monkey. (Actually, I have no idea if it is a capuchin monkey, but I am feeling kind of dumb right now, so I figured being specific about what type of monkey will improve my standing.)

On another bookcase, I was greeted with a proud, but wee, lion. "How did I not know that these figures were here?"

My wife sighed audibly and left for the downstairs, where there were, no doubt, more Red Rose beasties waiting upon her entrance.

My house is a preserve of tiny figurine creatures. I live amongst the wild beasts. I just wish I knew about it. I am curious what other things I haven't noticed. Husbands are stupid.

But I am a writer of disposable art, so I did my research. Thank you Internet!

The little figures are called Wade Whimsies. They started hanging out in boxes of Red Rose Tea in 1967 in Canada. We in America were not graced with such joy until 1983. There are not just animals. You might be blessed with a popular landmark in tiny glory. There are some that are just weird like one of the heads from Easter Island. A polar bear in your tea is charming and worth keeping. An ancient totem from a Pacific Island? Yeah. That's a tosser.

My wife has them because they remind her of her grandmother. She bought them at thrift stores and antique marts for a couple bucks each. This is an affordable way to keep memories alive. We are always trying to bring back those who are missing. If you can do that with a wee snow leopard that you got for less than a king sized candy bar, then you are living your best life.

But most people who have them got them from the Red Rose Tea box. I don't know if people bought the tea just for the figures, but it's a nice thing to find in a box of something you were going to have anyway. I like tea. I like small ceramic figurines. There is nothing wrong with getting something for nothing.

And that something is easy to place on a shelf. They are so small and unobtrusive. You can be like me, living with them for years unaware. I lived with animals? I did?

But that is the joy of little things. Now I am aware of them. Now I walk around the house and see the things I didn't know were there. The other life forms. Maybe I will be more aware of things in general. Maybe I will not trip over my winter boots. Maybe I will finally find those spare keys I have been looking for.

No doubt, the little yorkie figurine took them and hid them away in his miniature lair. Maybe that's where all the socks went too. Blame the Wade Whimsies. They are everywhere.

Twenty-One: Old Receipts (Left on the Curb)

Last Monday, I was heading into Nick's for the Monday Trivia when I saw Jeff picking up pieces of paper from the gutter of the street. Jeff is one of the regulars at Monday Trivia and I was not expecting him to be picking trash on such a lovely evening.

"Trash collector, your new vocation?" I asked.

Jeff looked up and gave me a smile of welcome. "Dave, there are all of these papers. They are old."

"Yeah, trash usually isn't new and shiny. Trash is mostly old. Mostly."

Jeff looked at me a little confused and then said, "Sure. But all of these papers are really old. Look," he said, holding up several pieces of paper. "These two are both dated 1970. That's pretty old."

I finally gazed at the curb and there were a few small piles of papers nestled by the tire of a car that just happened to be there. I leaned down and plucked up an invoice. I read it out to Jeff. It was a bill from Morse Brothers Electrical Company. The invoice date was January 20, 1970. It was sent to an insurance agency on Millbury Street. The insurance agency has been out of business for ages, though the sign still looms over the street.

We were joined by Mr. Dan who got into the swing of things and found some invoices of his own on the street. I read from the 51 year old invoice like it was some broken catechism. "In the work performed section they had typed Wire new lavatory. Install plugs. Wire commercial rate 20 gallon water heater. Wire meter trough and 60 amp MR switch."

We all got two or three letters and invoices in that little corner of Millbury Street. They were all dated 1970. I had a receipt of payment to Abbott Animal Hospital. It was marked paid 3/14/70. I wasn't aware of it, but Jeff and Mr. Dan informed me that Abbott was still in business. I wondered if they wanted their paperwork back. It was a little bit out of date, but it was still theirs.

What an odd site on Millbury Street. Three grown men picking up yellowed old pieces of paper from the dirty street and celebrating each scrap like it was a lost treasure. Like it told something important. I am sure the smart people of the neighborhood ignored we three maniacs.

Without saying it, we all picked a few of the old papers and kept them. We planned to hold on to them. We don't know why.

When we got into the bar, Sean the Bartender, rolled his eyes at us and asked, "What were you three knuckleheads doing dumpster diving in the middle of the street?"

We told him of our great discovery. We showed him the papers we now hoarded to us like Smiegel and his precious ring. He reiterated that we were idiots. We agreed. He then told us that he saw someone cleaning out the insurance agency office earlier in the day. The guy was carrying boxes of old papers out into a van.

It now made sense to us. This wasn't a strange wormhole we fell through. This was some papers from the 1970 box of receipts falling out onto the street when they were being loaded up. Well, maybe this is a kind of temporal wormhole.

These papers are worthless things. 51 years old. It tells of money owed, money paid. But I have found great joy in looking at them. I love how everything was typed out. All the itemized materials were painstakingly hunt and pecked through a typewriter. For the electrical invoice,we learned of the effort involved. They billed for ten and three quarters hours of labor. The electrician was worth nine dollars an hour. That's how much we pay for a licensed electrician now, right?

There is a story in these discarded pieces of commerce. Someone paid 22 dollars to have their animal looked at. Did it go well? Was it some daughter's beloved dog? Their cat? The receipt said the reference number for the transaction was 25,921. If we could look up the file, what stories might we discover?

For each of these invoices, these receipts, there are fragments of lives being lived. These invoices are tiny pinhole portals to gaze at half a century ago. But the holes are so small, we can barely see a thing. But that doesn't mean we shouldn't try to gaze back. To see the people who lived these receipts.

I am not advocating that we should gather up last week's CVS receipts and contemplate them like art on a museum wall. But let's not kid ourselves that these scraps of paper don't have stories to tell. They color in the blank areas of our collective memory. And they will be more pleasant clutter in my house, in my life.

And to any business looking for some old invoices, you can alway find Jeff, Mr. Dan or myself at Trivia most Mondays. We might have the old scraps you need.

Update: *Sad to say, by the time you read this, you will not have a chance to go to Nick's. It's last day is April 4th, 2022. It was a great place to hang out with friends or to sneak into the back booths and write. Just another scrap to flutter in the wind.*

Twenty-Two: Pine Cones

I was doing what I usually do, aimlessly wandering around a junk shop. I was just window shopping. Really, I am under strict orders from my wife to not bring home any junk shop stray I have absconded with. So I was just looking at all the lovely bits of refuse. And it appeared that I was also hearing the lovely refuse. I was hearing a conversation going on in a large wooden bowl. No one was around but me and all the junk. I leaned in close and saw that there were three pine cones in the bowl and they were having a heated conversation. I suppose all conversation between pine cones is always fiery. They didn't notice me, so I crouched down underneath the table made from a salvaged door and recorded their conversation on my phone.

First Pine Cone: Come on now, why do you think we are even in this bowl?

Second Pine Cone: Haven't I told you? Because it is decorative.

First Pine Cone: What do you mean, that we pine cones are decoration.

Second Pine Cone: You are twisting my words one more time. We are not decoration. We are part of an assemblage of disparate parts that are placed together, creating a heightened sense of pleasure for the design.

First Pine Cone: Three pine cones tossed in a fifty year old wooden bowl? That's a thing of the art of design? But they do. They place a bowl on table and put in pine cones. Who thought that was a good idea? And did anyone ask us if we wanted to participate in such a farce?

Second Pine Cone: We become the symbol of the connection to nature. They are never in a sterile home as long as there are some pieces of the forest in a bowl. We become the offering for a good, natural life.

First Pine Cone: And why us? Because we are cheap and plentiful. No one pays for a pine cone at a craft super store. You just go and pick them up from the ground. We are the road kill of the home decor world.

And the homeowner feels good because they made something earthy and homespun and didn't have to spend any money at Pottery Barn.

Second Pine Cone: Can't we be beautiful both in nature and in a nice table display?

First Pine Cone: Nature. We are holders of seeds. We are made to propagate the pine tree, not to be pretty to look at it.

Third Pine Cone: I agree, we aren't things that should just be looked at and gazed upon. We have the chance to get out of this wooden bowl prison and make a difference with kids. We can work together and have the children learn so much.

First Pine Cone: Are you talking about pre-school crafts. I thought that they stopped doing that to us due to allergies.

Third Pine Cone: You mean the pine cone bird feeders? What a great activity. Have the children spread peanut butter on our appendages and then cover the peanut butter with bird seed. Hang us on a tree and then watch in amazement as the birds peck at us.

Second Pine Cone: That is so barbaric. We are smeared in peanut butter and set upon by birds? What nightmare world did we awaken in?

First Pine Cone: That nightmare world has a name. It is kindergarten. Hear that word and tremble in fear.

Second Pine Cone: But they don't use us that way. Not because they are concerned with us, but that peanut butter now causes distress in some children. We are saved due to the sudden influx of nut allergies.

Third Pine Cone: First off, there was nothing wrong with being a bird feeder. It's a useful act. And second, just because we are not that anymore doesn't mean that we are needed in the STEM based classroom.

First Pine Cone: What, are we STEM teachers now? Does that mean we are in the teacher's union?

Third Pine Cone: Don't be ridiculous. We are used in a variety of projects. Because we are cheap and easily found, we are used often. Don't think of it as being misused, but that our ubiquity has made us essential to the learning process.

First Pine Cone: And how have we done such a thing while stuck in a wooden bowl in a junk shop?

Third Pine Cone: There is so much fun that we can be part of. They can learn so much about nature through us. In one they put three pine cones, like us, in three jars. One is just air. One has the pine cone in cold water. The third has the pine cone in hot water. The kids get to observe what changes occur. And do you know what they see?

First Pine Cone: I don't care what they learn. How can you think about what the kids learn when two of our pine cone brethren are drowned in jars of water? That is so barbaric.

Third Pine Cone: Okay. So you don't like learning science. How about art? They can paint with us. They can paint us and glue us together to make a wreath. Or with pipe cleaners, we turn into a halloween spider. Or we can be an owl. It's amazing what transformation awaits us in the art area of a preschool class. I feel honored by all the attention.

Second Pine Cone: The attention of turning into something we never were meant to be? No thank you. Just put me in a bowl and a let me be beautiful on my own.

First Pine Cone: Just leave me on the ground. Let me be part of the forest carpet. Like I was always meant to be.

Third Pine Cone: Where's the fun in that?

First Pine Cone: I won't be able to explain it to you if you just don't get it.

And realizing that the junk shop owner was looking at me sideways, I decided that I didn't get it either, and left without making a purchase.

Twenty Three: QSL Cards

Sometimes, when you enter the Library of Disposable Art, you can look at what's there and get it right away. "Hey, that's a T-Shirt." Or "Look at those cute ceramic animals that came from the tea box." You can understand what they are and figure out for yourself if it is cool or not. Then there are some alcoves in the library that have items that make a fella scratch their head in confusion. What the hell is this and why do people collect them?

And this is not me attacking the lovers of Hummel figurines (though I just don't get that one bit. Those are nightmare inducing totems.). No, this is not about your personal taste, but things that you look at and don't understand and when someone explains it to you, you still don't understand. It's like we are suffering from bric-a brac aphasia.

That is the case with QSL cards. I have a zine that reproduces authentic QSL cards from Washington State during the 1970s. You see. I wrote the words using as much English as I ever was taught, and yet the damn sentence does not make much sense. But just because it is odd for myself and you (probably) does not mean that somewhere in town, there are several people with large collections of these aforementioned QSL cards.

What are QSL cards? I'm glad you asked. Actually, I have been dreading this part of the column. The part where I explain what I am going on about. I have never been an ace at making myself clear (see earlier essays in the series to prove my point.) And I feel like I might not make much sense (so what else is new?). But here goes.

When people communicate to each other through Ham Radio or through CB radio, they will reach one person somewhere in the globe. That is the purpose. To contact another lover of Ham or CB. To reach somewhere you never have reached before.

When you do have contact with someone, the routine is to send a QSL card to a central processing center and they will then send the card to the other person involved in the conversation. The QSL card has the user's personal information on it. It will also give details of the contact the two users had. This card means, "I acknowledge this transmission." People collect these cards to show where all the people they spoke to over their radio were. They try to get cards delivered from as far as possible.

The cards themselves can be plain postcards with just the info printed on it. But in the peak of the CB craze in the 70s, the cards became illustrated. They had funny cartoons on them. They had pictures. There were people who made a living drawing QSL card cartoons. They are a little bit folk art, a little bit underground comix and a touch of "what the hell is this."

I was going through the zine that had all of these examples of QSL cards and an old friend confessed he was getting his Ham Radio license. He told me that he loves QSL cards. He still gets them. He is in the process of creating the image for his own card, which will be an aerial photo of his hometown.

This blew me away. The idea that people still do this is crazy to me. That they still use Ham radios to communicate with and use postcards to acknowledge that moment of contact with another. Yesterday, I spoke to a co-worker in Oaxaca, Mexico. I picked up my mobile phone and we chatted about work for a half hour. While it was sleeting here in New England, he described the 75 degree weather he was afforded outside his house in the mountains. Do we need Ham radio to shrink the world? Do we need kitschy postcards to say that, "I am here. And for a moment, we spoke together over a radio. Are we here together?"

And for some of us, the answer is yes. Yes. I need to talk to someone outside of Zoom and unlimited minutes. I need to put some effort in the act of reaching out. I need to get something in the mail, something that was touched by many hands, to say that we are all here together.

The world is a lot smaller than we ever thought it would be. But we need to put some effort into it. We need funny postcards sent to us, to remind us of the world that is all around us. We need someone to say to us, in the friendliest tone possible, "I acknowledge this transmission."

Update: *Just another thank you to one of my dearest and oldest friends. Foster really got me to understand the whole concept of the QSL card. If there is still confusion while reading, the fault is mine. He explained it to me with kindness and clarity. Foster told me he tried to get the aerial photo for QSL card, but it didn't turn out well, so he went for another image of his town.*

Twenty Four: Cell Animation

When I picked up my cell animation from Framed in Tatnuck, I gave my name and the woman said, "Oh you had the animated dragon."

For some ridiculous reason, I took offense at this. "No. That's not a dragon. That's Godzooki." The woman, a trained framing professional, looked at me like I was a crazy person.

I was worse than a crazy person, I was a collector of nostalgia. There is nothing more annoying. If you get something wrong about my collection, I will have to correct you in the snootiest way possible.

Let's stop here for a moment. There is a lot to unpack in the first hundred words of this column.

What is cell animation? That's a piece of the process animators used to make cartoons. For every second of cartoon goodness on Saturday morning, they had to paint the characters in progressively different poses at least fifteen times. For really good animation, like Disney movies, there would be 24 cells of animation drawn and painted. For TV animation, there would be something like 14 to 18 cells.

The cells are sheets of clear celluloid. The animation team would paint an image on each one. They would then put the cell on a pre-painted background and shoot it on one frame of film. They would then take that off the background and put the next frame on and repeat the whole process. It took thousands of drawings to create a half hour episode of the Smurfs or the Care Bears (the classics). This process has been superseded by computer animation processes. There is no need for cell animation. But that does not mean the cells of past cartoons are gone for good.

The reams and reams of cells were thrown out or left to rot in warehouses. They are now bought by weird guys who want to remember their childhood. They want a piece of their childhood. I know of one animation collector who amasses all the cells from the X-Men cartoon from the 90s. He can look at a cell and tell you what episode it was drawn for. I guess it pays to be a savant if you want to collect obscure elements of antiquated animation methodology.

For the most part, because there were so many cells created, they don't have a huge monetary value. You want some Bugs Bunny cells? That will cost you. If you are in the market for Strawberry Shortcake animation, you might not break the bank. They are berry affordable.

The other piece of information you will need is, who is Godzooki. When I was a Saturday morning cartoon devotee, in the 70s, there was a Godzilla cartoon show. Godzilla was a good guy, saving the world from giant monsters. But you can't just have a giant monster to sell sugar cereal, you need a funny sidekick. Godzooki was born. He was a diminutive relative to Godzilla who was silly and always underfoot. Oh, that Godzooki. He even made it into the theme song. He was legit. I thought he was great, though if he is recalled, it is with derision. He is the Scrappy Doo of the Kaiju world.

And I have several cell animations of him. The cells show a great deal of work. They were never meant to be loved for themselves. They were always part of a whole, of a cartoon. But this is how you can get close to the shows you love. You can own the smallest of parts.

I have a small collection. I have some Ewoks cells and a Charlie Brown cell that was part of a Chex cereal commercial. They are fun. They are a reminder that entertainment takes many steps and many hands.

But I think I am being a bad collector. I read that I am not storing them correctly. They are made from celluloid. They can deteriorate. They will start to break down and a strong vinegar odor will come from your disposable art piece. There is a name for this, it is called Vinegar Syndrome. It is deadly to the cell. But I'm not concerned. My cells are smelling fine, for now.

But that's the thing with disposable art. Do we want these to last forever? Is art meant to be eternal? Is the art that brings nostalgia even worth preserving for the greater world? Or do we all know that soon we too will turn brown and blurry and smell of vinegar? Will all the memories of our childhood ooze into simpler parts? And who will sing the praises of Godzooki then?

Appendix

The column is still going. I am very honored to be in such a magazine as Worcester Magazine. When I first moved to the Worcester area, this was the magazine I would pick up to see what was going on in the city I was adopting. It makes me proud that I now am one of the voices in those pages.

Once again, I want to thank Victor Infante for letting me write about silly things we don't throw away. We imprint meaning and worth on these things and that is worth exploring and celebrating.

Victor has also been kind to invite me into a few other projects for the magazine. One of them is for "The Rest of Worcester" feature. He asked a variety of writers to come up with fake superlatives about our city. I submitted five entries into the feature.

These little pieces seem to be adjacent to what I have been writing about in my column, so I thought it would be nice to share them here.

The Best Worcester Restaurant I Never Ate At - Jekyll and Hyde Burrito on Park Ave

It was around 2000. I was hungry and went into the first sandwich shop I found. The place was empty. The people behind the counter were putting things in boxes. I asked if I could get a burrito. One of them shouted, "Does it look like you can get a burrito? We are out of business. Why didn't you come here earlier and we wouldn't be broke." I left, wondering which one he was: Jekyll or Hyde.

Best Street to Admire the Nip Bottles in the Gutter - Millbury Street

If you keep your eyes down while walking this historic boulevard, you will be treated by a glittering display of art and desire. It glitters in the sun. You will see a variety of nip bottles on the ground, gathering together to tell an exciting tale of abandon and despair. The amazing thing about it, is that this art installation is always growing. There are many volunteers contributing to the piece by downing and dropping a new bottle on the concrete canvas. Another brushstroke of genius. Be careful where you step. Art is everywhere.

The Best Mural That is No Longer Present Advertising a Business That is Also No Longer Around - Heidi's Hippie Hideaway

For years, while driving on 290, I would see the quaintly illustrated mural for Heidi's and be filled with joy and hope. The idea that Worcester had such an Eden was groovy. Every time I saw the mural I was enticed with pulling off the highway and checking it out. What kind of bar or coffee shop would be so perfectly named? In fact, the store was a thrift shop and it was out of business for many years. Now the mural is also absent and our chance to make Worcester a hippie paradise is fading like so much sandblasted paint.

Best Reason to Consider Moving from Your Current Apartment -The Neighbors

Having a beer with an off duty police officer, I mentioned my address. The off duty police officer became animated and said, "Oh, I know that building. That's right next to that place where we busted those guys who were setting up a bomb making operation. We got them. You don't have to worry anymore. Drink your beer."

The Best Indicator that Business in Worcester is Tough - The Ripped Grand Opening Sign on Pleasant Street.

There on Pleasant, is the hulk of a general store. The name is not clear. In the window is half of a Grand Opening sign. It seems that someone attempted to rip it off, but only got a rough half of it removed. It is there to remind you how close the Grand Opening is to the Going Our of Business. There are so many questions. Was it open for a very short time? Did they just forget to take the Grand Opening sign off? Could they have just moved to a better location? And is anything ever going to go into that space?

Acknowledgements

In addition to the wonderful support of Victor Infante, I want to thank those who helped with the writing of these columns. Many gave me ideas or story sparks and I am grateful. In no order, thanks go to, Sean, Heather, George, Foster, Jeff, the other Jeff, Chris, Deb, Paul, Mr. Dan, Bruce, Tom, Amanda, Ken, Jesse, Jonathan. If I forgot anyone, it is because I am a doofus.

About the Book

What do you collect?

What is hanging around the house with you like an old friend?

This is a book about all the things in our lives that we keep even though we know better. What are the things we should throw away, but we hold on to? Can we see the collection of playbills from local community theater productions art? If it isn't art, what is it?

In this book, there are chapters that look at coloring books, t-shirts, collectible Star Wars glasses, celebrity autographs, and so much more.

Collecting the first two years of popular column published in the Worcester Magazine, The Library of Disposable Art is a funny, kind hearted look at the things we can't part with. The things we find beauty in, though no one else does. The things that define us.

About the Writer

Dave has written nearly 100 books that have been released electronically. They span the gamut from fiction to memoir to really weird shit. He has been lucky to be a columnist for Worcester Magazine. All of his books are available to purchase on a variety of sites. All of them are cheap and relatively short. Who wants to overstay their welcome?

The Library of Disposable Art

This is the series of books that I assembled to look at pop culture. When I needed a column idea, I figured that there are topics that can't support a full book. So the column got the same name. But what are the books? Well, here they are.

1 - Mama Cass's Golden Caramel Bar. This was a look at one episode of the Scooby Doo New Movies. It is, of course, the one with Mama Cass as the guest star. You know the one, they are stuck in a haunted candy factory. There is a lot of running around and eating of candy.

2- Orphan Store Signs. I mention this book in one of the columns. It was a chance for me to wander around Worcester County and record all the signs for businesses that are no longer there, but the signs are.

3- Are You a True Life Form? Perry Rhodan is a very popular character. In Germany, there have been over three thousand novels written about him and his world. This book looks at that while I read eight of the translated books.

4- In This Reality. I watched the Tom Petty video, You Got Lucky, and wrote a chapter about each second of the video.

5- Lon Chaney is Innocent. Lon Chaney, Jr. made six films under the Inner Sanctum brand. In the movies, his character is usually accused of a heinous crime. I go through these movies in the way Chaney would have, drunk.

6- And If You Stare Into the Garbage Pail, The Garbage Pail Also Stares Into You. Wow. That's a title. This one has me staring at a vintage pack of Garbage Pail Kids Stickers for three hours and writing about my ideas and thoughts.